BLACK'S PICTURE INFORMATION BOOKS

Scientific Adviser Jean Imrie MSc, Area Adviser, West Riding CC

trees

CLARE WILLIAMS

Adam and Charles Black · London

Published by A & C Black Ltd
4, 5 & 6 Soho Square, London W1V 6AD

© 1970 Moussault's Uitgeverij NV, Amsterdam
© 1972 (English edition) A & C Black Ltd

ISBN 0 7136 1279 7

Printed in the Netherlands by Ysel Press, Deventer

First published in the Netherlands by Moussault's
Uitgeverij NV under the title *Bomen en struiken*, with
a text by G den Hoed; this text translated by
Adrienne Dixon and comprehensively adapted by
Clare Williams with the help of Jean Imrie.

Acknowledgements

The illustrations in this book are by Ebbe Sunesen,
Preben Dahlstrom, E Hahnewald and Henning Anthon.

The photographs are reproduced by courtesy of: A-Z
Botanical Collections Ltd page 56; Big Farm Manage-
ment page 54; A D S Macpherson page 55, and
P F White page 49.

The colour illustrations are reproduced by kind per-
mission of Eyre Methuen Ltd, London, publishers of
Helge Vedel & Johan Lange's *Trees and bushes in wood
and hedgerow*.

Foreword

Britain was once a land of great forests, stretching right across the country. Over the centuries nearly all this forest land was cleared for farming; the wood was used for building ships, houses and furniture, and for pit-props for the old coal mines.

Trees take a long time to grow. Even a fast-growing tree takes eighty years to reach its full height, and there are oak trees in Britain which were acorns when the Romans were here. When people plant trees, it is always a long-term project—not for their own generation but for the future; and likewise, we have to think carefully before we cut down trees, because they are not easily replaced.

Why do we want trees in the first place? The first reason is perhaps that they are attractive. Tree-lined streets keep cities from being 'brick and concrete jungles'. The seasonal changes give the street a feeling of natural life. In the country trees form an important part in the pattern of the countryside, both in woods and forests and in the hedgerows, where they act as windbreaks.

Wood is also needed for timber, for pulp, and for paper-making. We import most of the wood we use for these purposes, but the Forestry Commission is trying to produce more home-grown wood.

This book will help you identify the commoner trees, and will tell you about each species. It will also give you general information about the structure and uses of wood, and about the flowering, fruiting and growth of trees.

To help you identify a tree, there are pictures of the leaves of each species, the fruits and the silhouette, or outline, of the tree. When you think you have identified it, you can turn to the colour pictures to check all the other details.

Contents

Tree silhouettes

1. SCOTS PINE
(max. height 40 m)

5. YEW
(max. height 10 m)

3. EUROPEAN LARCH
(max. height 35 m)

2. NORWAY SPRUCE
(max. height 45 m)

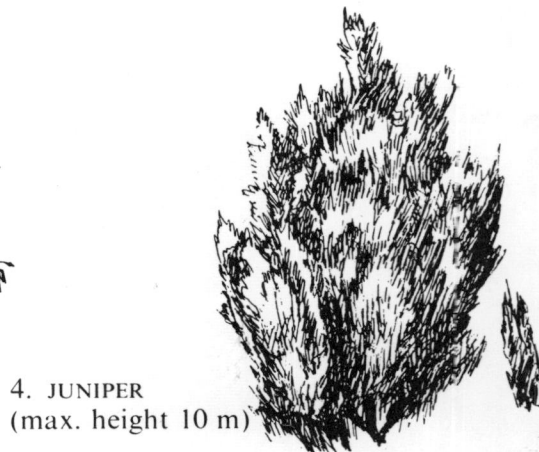

4. JUNIPER
(max. height 10 m)

6. ASPEN
(max. height 24 m)

7. BLACK ITALIAN POPLAR
(max. height 20 m)

7. POLLARDED TREE,
either a poplar
or a willow (9–10 m)

IO

8. WHITE POPLAR, OR ABELE
(max. height 30 m)

10. COMMON OSIER
(max. height 25 m)

9. GOAT WILLOW
(max. height 9 m)

11–12. BIRCH
(max. height 20 m)

16. HORNBEAM
(max. height 12 m)

17. BEECH
(max. height 30 m)

13–14. ALDER
(max. height 24 m)

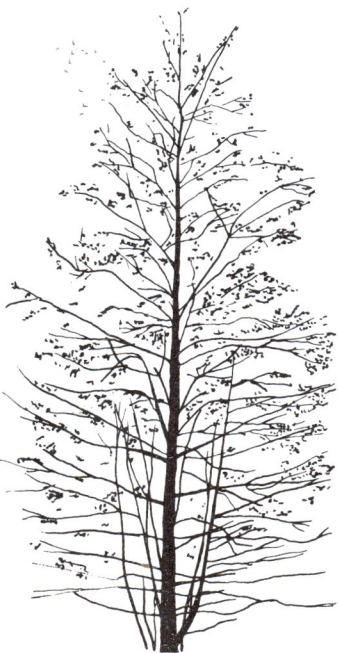

15. HAZEL
(max. height 6 m)

12

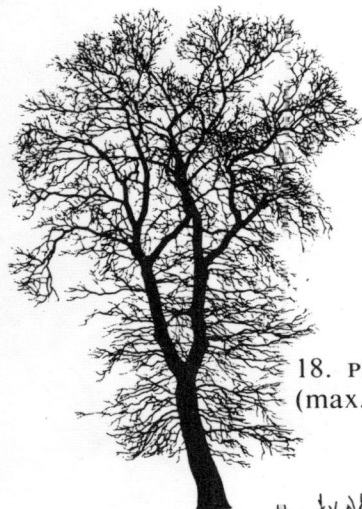

18. PEDUNCULATE OAK
(max. height 30 m)

20. RED OAK
(max. height 25 m)

22. HAWTHORN
(max. height 7 m)

21. ELM
(max. height 35 m)

19. SESSILE OAK
(max. height 30 m)

13

23. ROWAN
(max. height 9 m)

26. HOLLY
(max. height 10 m)

28. ACACIA
(max. height 25 m)

14

29. SYCAMORE
(max. height 16 m)

30. HORSE CHESTNUT
(max. height 20 m)

31. LIME
(max. height 30 m)

I5

33. COMMON ELDER
(max. height 6 m)

32. ASH
(max. height 40 m)

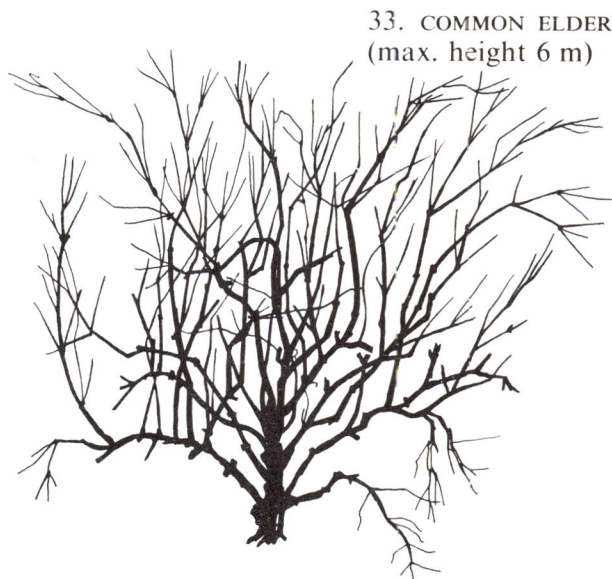

34. GUELDER ROSE
(max. height 3 m)

Leaf shapes

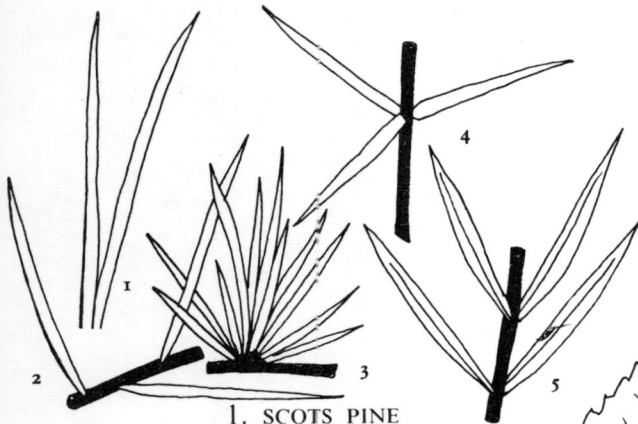

1. SCOTS PINE
2. NORWAY SPRUCE
3. EUROPEAN LARCH
4. JUNIPER
5. YEW

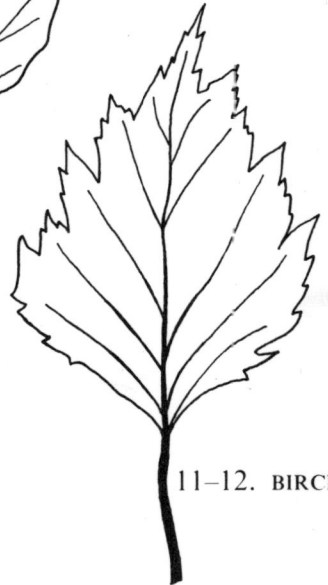

6. ASPEN

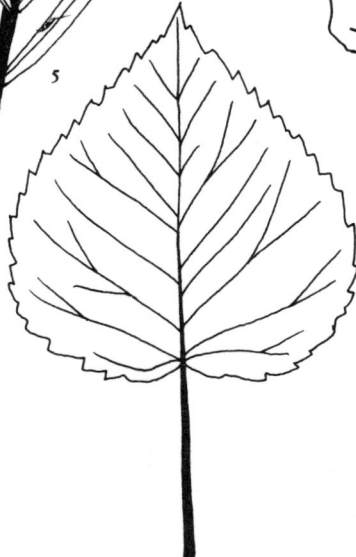

7. BLACK ITALIAN POPLAR

11–12. BIRCH

8. WHITE POPLAR

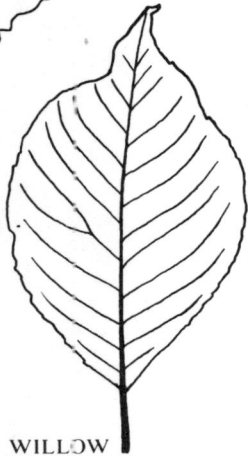

9. GOAT WILLOW

10. COMMON OSIER

10. WHITE WILLOW

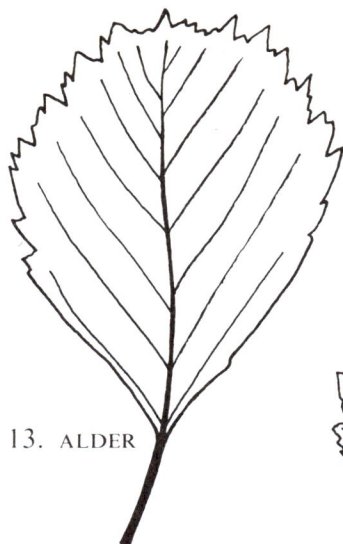

13. ALDER

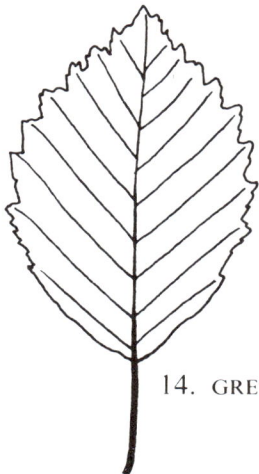

14. GREY ALDER

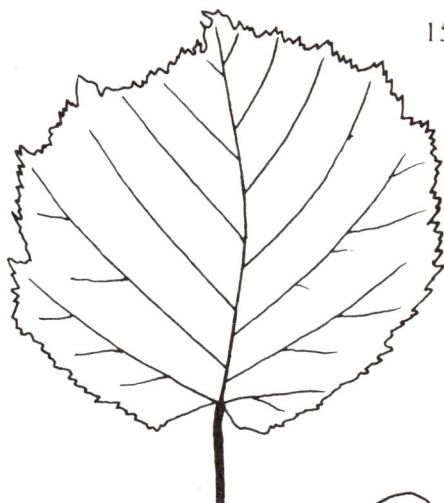

15. HAZEL

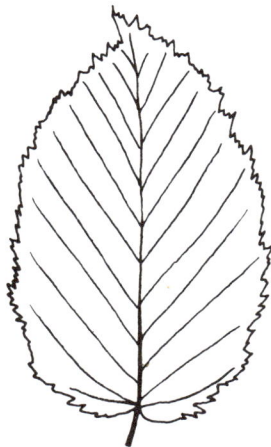

16. HORNBEAM

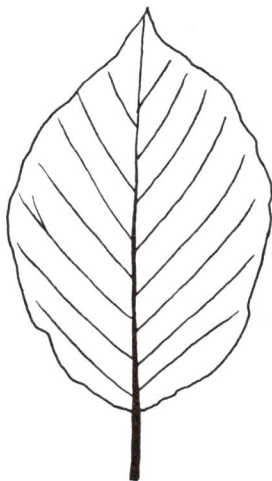

17. BEECH

18. PEDUNCULATE OAK

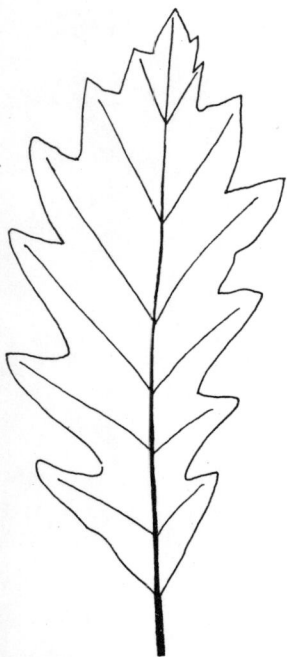

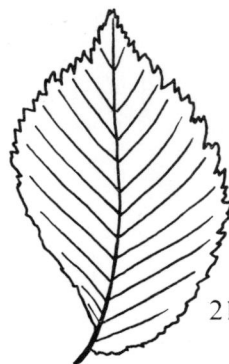

21. WYCH ELM

19. SESSILE OAK

20. RED OAK

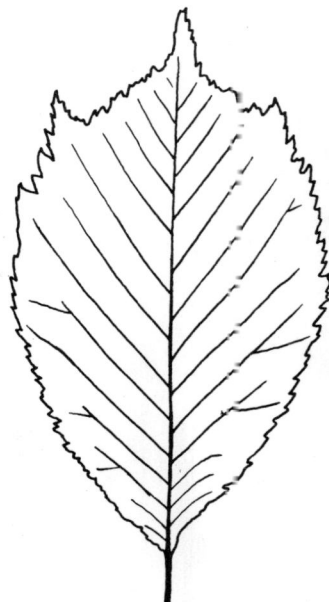

21. FLUTTERING ELM

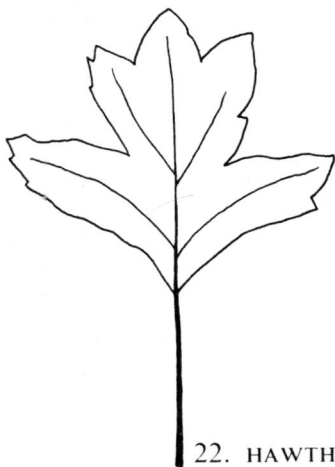

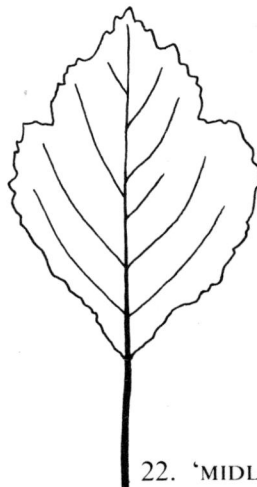

23. ROWAN

22. HAWTHORN

22. 'MIDLAND' HAWTHORN

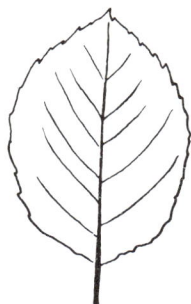

24. MEDLAR

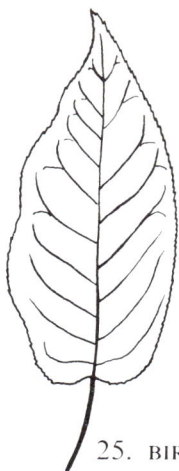

25. BIRD CHERRY

26. HOLLY

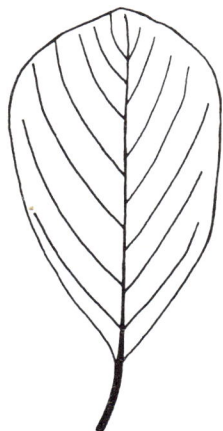

27. ALDER
BUCKTHORN

28. ACACIA

29. SYCAMORE

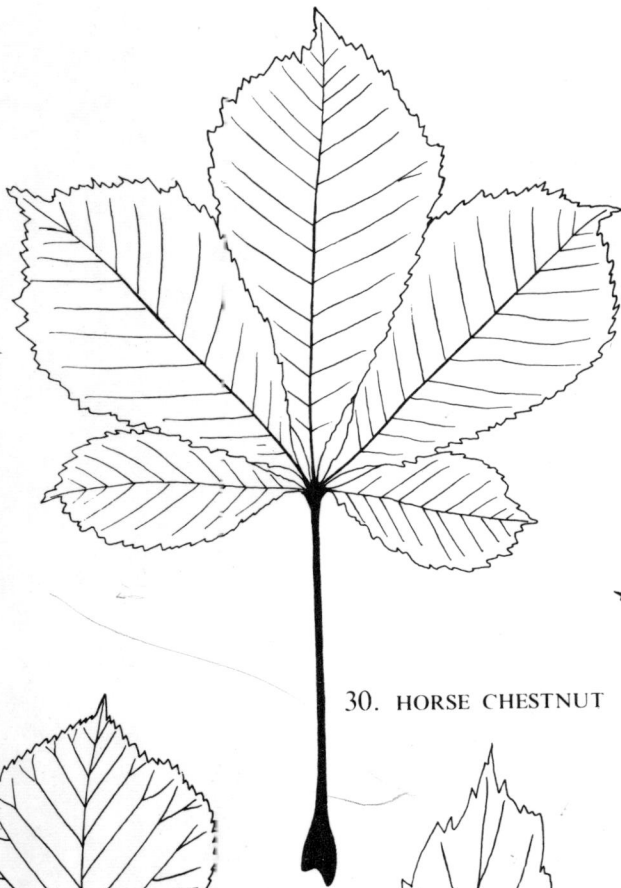

30. HORSE CHESTNUT

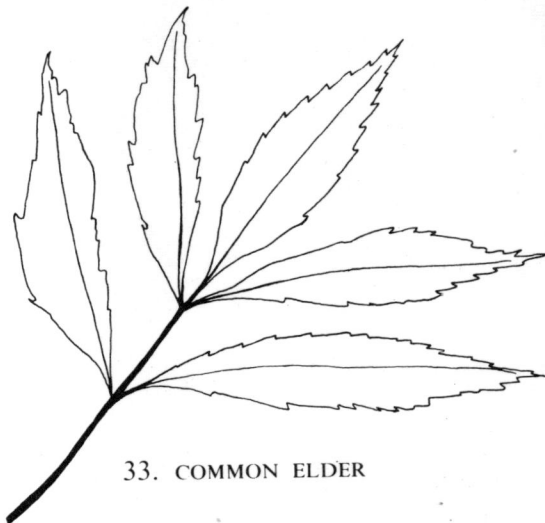

33. COMMON ELDER

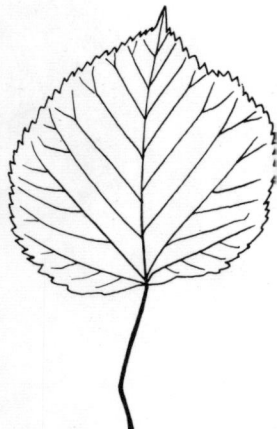

32. ASH

31. LIME

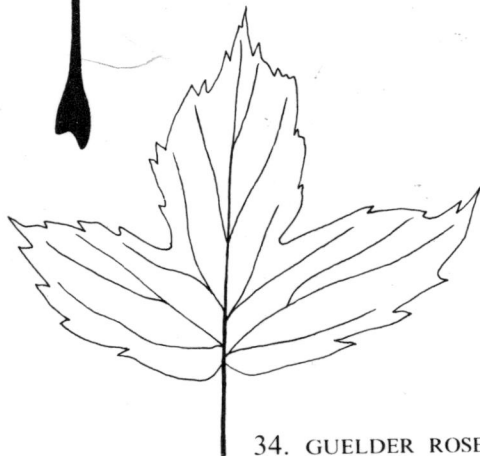

34. GUELDER ROSE

Fruits

1. SCOTS PINE

3. EUROPEAN LARCH

2. NORWAY SPRUCE

5. YEW

6–10. POPLARS AND WILLOWS

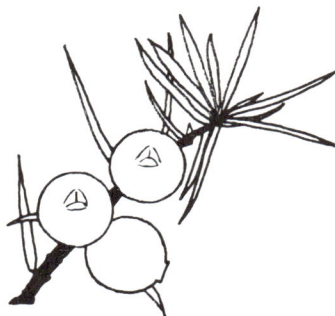

4. JUNIPER

11–12. BIRCHES

6–10. POPLARS AND WILLOWS

15. HAZEL

13–14. ALDERS

16. HORNBEAM

17. BEECH

18–20. OAKS

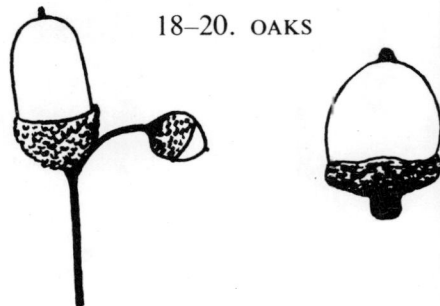

21. ELM

22. HAWTHORN

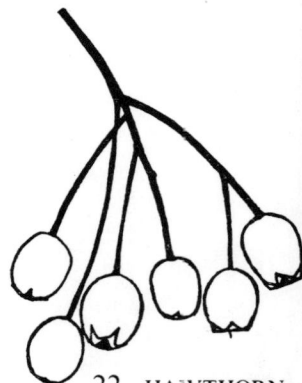

24. MEDLAR

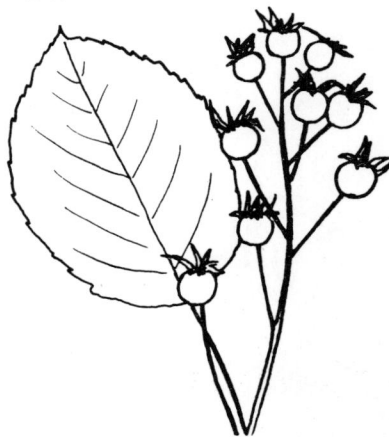

23. ROWAN

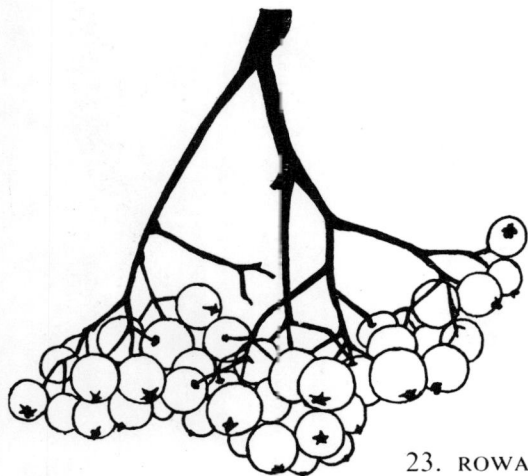

25. BIRD CHERRY

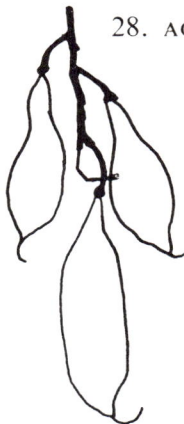

28. ACACIA

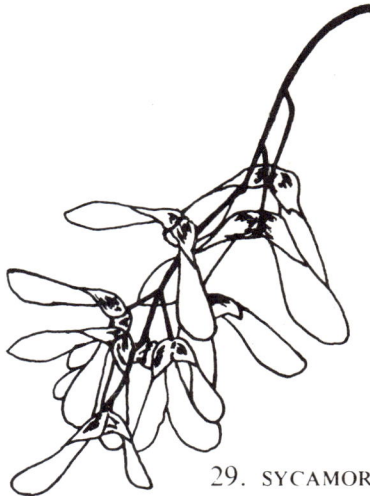

29. SYCAMORE

30. HORSE CHESTNUT

26. HOLLY

27. ALDER BUCKTHORN

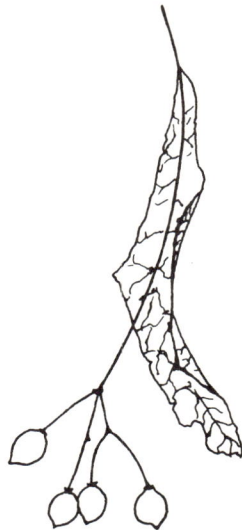

31. LIME

23

32. ASH

33. COMMON ELDER

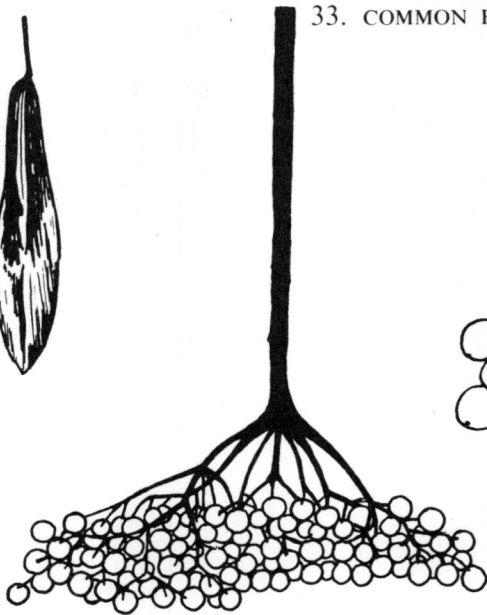

34. GUELDER ROSE

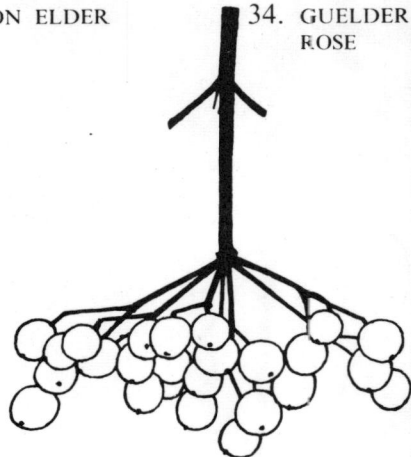

1. Scots pine *Pinus sylvestris*

This grows everywhere in Britain but is commonest in Scotland. It can grow on poor, sandy soil. Because the needle-leaves give little shade, there will be a good deal of undergrowth which makes a good place for animals to live in. The undergrowth and the long tree-roots stop the soil being washed away by rain.

Flowering Scots pines are 5–40 m high. In a sheltered position the trunk grows straight, but in a windy place the tree may be twisted and the branches crooked.

The needle-shaped leaves are placed in pairs, each pair within a shallow socket (1f). The older needles die and fall off at all times of year.

Flowering is in May–June. Below the tips of the twigs are clusters of male flowers (1b), which release fine dry pollen. Most of it is wasted, but some reaches the female cones, which are found at the tips of the twigs (1c). These then become hard green 'fircones'. A year later, the cone scales have become wooden and brown (1d). In dry weather the scales bend outwards (1e); the winged seeds inside fall, and are spread about by the wind. In damp weather the cones close up.

The bark is thick and brown at the foot of the tree, and cracks as the tree grows. Higher up, the bark is reddish-brown and peels off easily.

When the trunk of the Scots pine is straight, it can be used for telegraph poles, etc. Sawn pine-wood makes good timber for carpentry.

clusters of stamens (2d) release great quantities of pollen, so that the ground below may be quite yellow and much is wasted.

The fertilised cones become long and pendulous (2e). The scales are flexible. Squirrels often eat the winged seeds inside the cone (2f) and leave the cone lying on the ground.

The wood is called deal. It contains many knots and streaks of resin, but it is cheap because the tree grows fast. Much of it is used for paper, cardboard, and softboard.

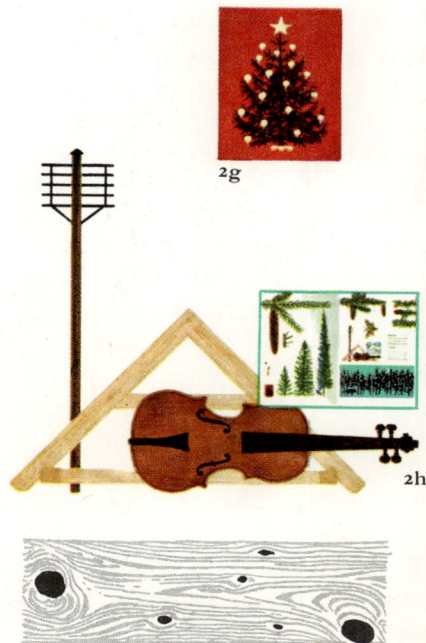

2. Norway spruce *Picea abies*

The Norway spruce is our Christmas tree (2g). There are several varieties of spruce, none of them native to Britain. They are planted here because the wood is very useful. Not much light gets through to the ground in spruce forests, so there is not much undergrowth. The roots do not go very deep, and spruces are often blown down in gales. They can grow up to 50 m high.

The needles of the spruce are placed singly (2b) and are very sharp. Young branches are smooth and yellowish brown, getting darker as they grow older.

Flowering is in May. The female flowers (not easy to see, because they are high up) are red cones (2c). The male, egg-shaped

Deal contains many knots

3. European larch *Larix decidua*

The larch is deciduous. Its needles begin to turn yellow in September, and a month later they have all fallen off. The tree grows up to 35 m (3a). In April tufts of young green needles appear on wart-like short branches (3b). They never become as hard (3e) as those of pines and spruces.

Here and there the short branches produce flowers. The male flowers contain only stamens (3c). The female flowers grow on longer shoots; they have purple bracts or scales (3d). These will eventually become the seed cones, which are at first brown (3f) and stay on the branches for years (3g). By then the seeds have fallen out.

Pollination and seed dispersal are by wind, but not many seeds germinate. Larches usually have to be planted. Unfortunately some varieties of larch are attacked by a disease called 'larch canker', which can kill the tree.

The wood is yellowish, with a reddish-brown heart.

4a

4d

4b

4c

5d

5c

5a

5b

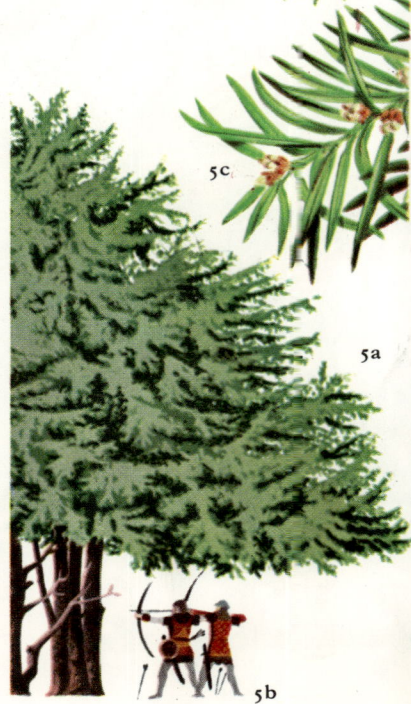

hills of southern England. Dwarf junipers (less than 1 m high) grow in the north of Scotland.

4. Juniper *Juniperus communis*

This shrub-like tree, between 0·5 and 10 m high, is an evergreen. It has short, sharp needles, placed in whorls of three round the branches. It flowers in May. On one plant there are either male flowers (4b) or female cones (4c). After fertilisation, the female cones become plump and fleshy. After the winter they turn dark blue, and are used to flavour gin (4d).

The wood is tough but soft. It is used for good quality wood-work. The tree is found mainly in Scotland and on the chalk

5. Yew *Taxus baccata*

This evergreen grows to a height of 2 to 10 m and has flat needles which are neither hard nor sharp. The wood was once used for making longbows, and now it is used by wood-carvers.

It flowers in March–April. Male (5c) and female flowers (5d, left) are not found on the same plant. The seed is very strange: it can be seen from the outside, but a wine-red juicy coat fits round it like a cap (5d). Birds eat this and drop the seed. Both leaves and seeds are poisonous to animals.

6. Aspen *Populus tremula*

'Trembling like an aspen leaf' is a common saying. If we look at an aspen, we can see why. The leaves rustle in the slightest wind, probably because of the broad leaf and thin leaf-stalk (6a).

Aspen grows on sandy soil to a height of 6–24 m. The tips of the uppermost branches have pointed buds, and are covered with scars of leaves which have fallen off (6e).

Flowering is in March–April, before there are any leaves. Trees are either male or female. The male flowers are found in a light red catkin (6d), and the female catkins (6b) are green. The female catkins become fruiting catkins; these contain silky hairs, which help the seeds to float away in the wind. In autumn the leaves turn beautiful colours, from golden yellow to purple.

The roots are shallow, but there are many of them. The wood is light and airy. Because it splits and frays easily it is used for making matches (6f), and also high-grade paper.

7c   8b

7. Black Italian poplar
Populus serotina

This is a cross between the European and American black poplars. The Lombardy poplar is closely related to it.

Lombardy and Black Italian poplars are nearly all male trees, and they are reproduced by planting cuttings. The male flowers appear in April–May (7b). The leaves are triangular to heart-shaped (7a). The tree can be recognised by its shape (7c), and because it is still bare when other trees already have fresh leaves.

Because the tree grows fast, it is often planted along new roads. It makes an excellent windbreak along motorways.

7a

7b

8. White poplar, or abele
Populus alba

The underside of the leaves is covered in silvery-white hairs, which gives the tree its name. Both male and female trees are found, and the seeds are spread by the wind. The leaves are palmate (8a).

White poplars grow fast, up to 30 m in height. They are often planted as ornamental trees and, because they stand up well to salty air, are often grown near the coast.

8a

9. Goat willow *Salix caprea*

Willows are also known in Britain as withies, sallows, osiers and saughs. It is difficult to tell the varieties apart, because the same variety can be a tree, a bush, or a *pollarded* tree (see page 9). There are many cross strains between different willows. Some goat willows have low hanging branches, but the true 'weeping willow' is the common osier.

The goat willow is easily recognised by its egg-shaped leaves (9b) with grey and hairy undersides (9c). The young shoots are downy too. The tree grows to a height of 3–9 m.

Catkins appear in February–March (9a). Male and female catkins do not appear on the same tree. The female catkins look like green brushes; the male catkins are at first silky and white, and later light yellow because of the many stamens (9e). Both male and female catkins produce nectar, which attracts bees, wasps and flies. When the fruits burst open, they release a lot of down as well as seed. This helps in wind dispersal.

The wood is soft. The sapwood is yellowish, with a yellow-red heartwood.

10. Common osier and white willow *Salix alba*

These are the most common willows. They are found along roads, ditches and lakes, in marshes, by rivers and in parks.

The common osier can be recognised by its leaves (10a). These are long; the edges are curled and the underside is silvery-white. The branches and buds are covered with dense hair. The white willow has similar long leaves but with saw-toothed *(serrated)* edges and a silky underside (10b and c).

The weeping willow (10d) is a variety of white willow. Both the common osier and the white willow produce supple branches; these branches are lopped off ('pollarding') and used for basket-making and furniture-making (10e and f). A pollard is a mass of scars caused by pruning. Each year it can grow new branches as much as 2 m long.

One kind of white willow gives wood suitable for cricket bats.

10a

10e

10f

10c

10b

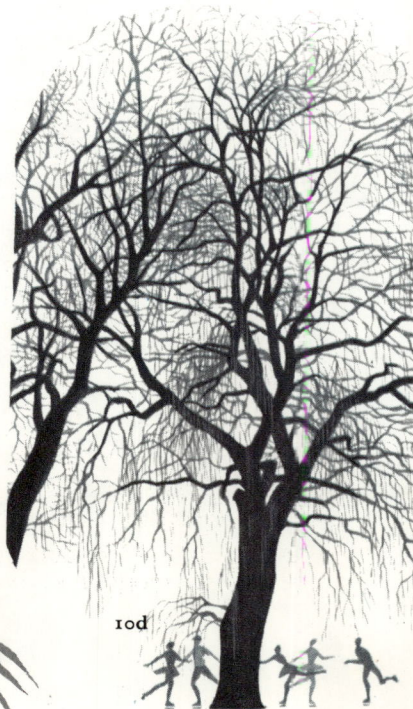
10d

11. Silver birch *Betula verrucosa*

This common tree grows to a height of 20 m. It can be recognised by its bark, which is at first smooth and brown, but becomes white and marked with spots as the tree gets older. The outer layers of bark peel off in papery strips.

The young leaves are covered with sticky resin. You can still see white resin flakes on older leaves. By mid-October the leaves will all have fallen, completely yellow.

Immediately after the leaves appear, flowering begins. The young male catkins (11a) begin to grow and release pollen. The female catkins (11b) become pendulous (11c). After fertilisation they separate into fruit and bracts (11d and e). The winged fruits are dispersed by the wind, leaving part of the catkin hanging on the tree.

12. Birch *Betula pubescens*

The branches are less flexible than those of the silver birch, and do not droop. The tree can be best recognised by the shape of the fruit (12a) and the scale (12b).

13. Alder *Alnus glutinosa*

This tree grows by the water-side, to a height of 24 m. Its shape is easily recognisable in winter (13a). The strong end buds produce both male and female catkins. The female catkins appear in summer, as small green knots. They last through the winter, and mature before the leaves appear (13b). The long dangling male catkins appear and shed pollen in the early spring (13d). When fertilised, the female catkins grow into plump balls (13c). Finally they become dry and black (13e), and the tiny fruits fall out. The fruits are dispersed by water or wind.

The freshly cut wood is yellowish white, but turns orange when exposed to air. It can be used for making plywood.

14. Grey alder *Alnus incana*

This alder does not require damp and fertile soil, so it is useful in forestry projects. It does not grow as high as the common alder. Flowering is earlier, but the leaves sprout later. The tree is easily recognised by the dry old female catkins (14) which have very short stalks.

13d
13e
14
13c
13b
13a

15. Hazel *Coryllus avellana*

Hazel is a bush, growing to a height of 3–6 m (15a). The branches spring straight from the ground. The leaves do not begin to appear until May, and do not fall till November. They are big and coarse (15b).

Flowering is in early spring. The male catkins (15c) sometimes lose all their pollen before the female catkins (15d) are out. In these years there will be few nuts. The fruits (15e) ripen in October into hazel nuts, which are eaten by animals.

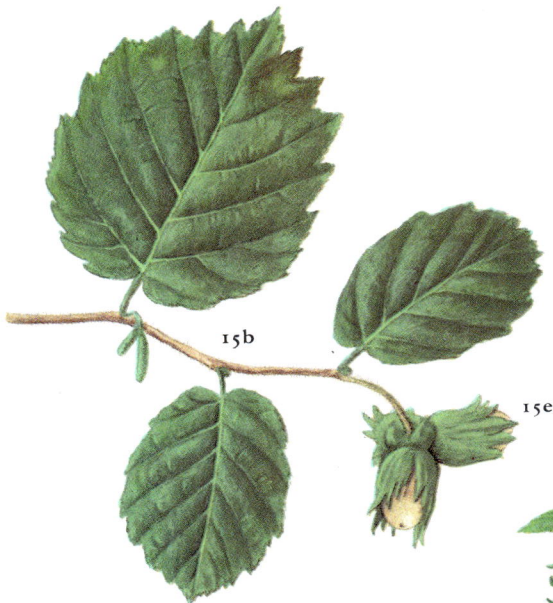

16. Hornbeam *Carpinus betulus*

Its light grey trunk looks rather like a beech, but it is not in the beech family. Hornbeam grows to a height of 12 m, and is often planted in parks.

The egg-shaped leaves have serrated edges (16a). They do not fall off the tree in winter, but just wither. Male and female catkins (16b and c) appear at the same time as the leaves. After fertilisation the female catkin becomes a cluster of fruits (16d), each with a persistent green bract.

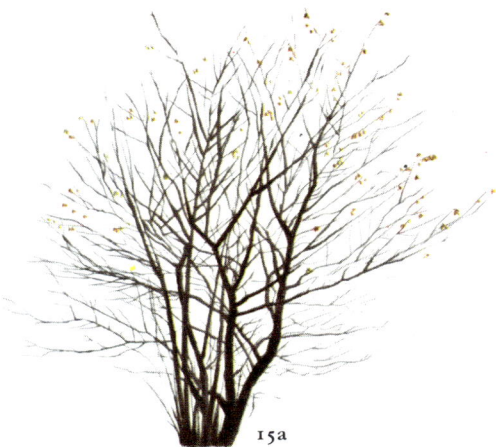

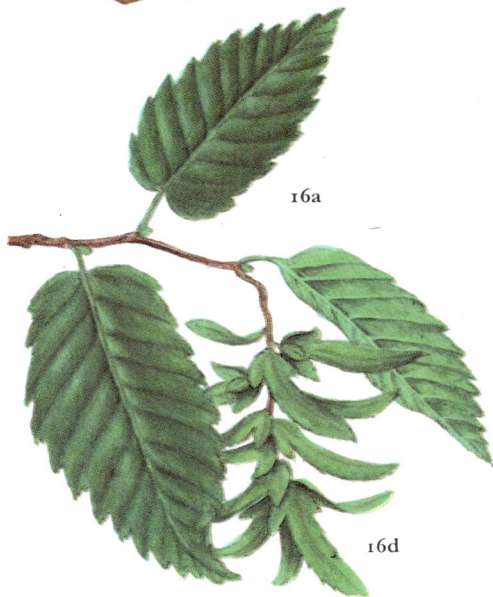

15a

15f

15d

15c

15b

15e

16a

16b

16c

16d

17. Beech *Fagus sylvatica*

One of the most important trees in British forestry, the beech grows to a height of over 30 m. In forests the trunk is straight and free of branches (17a).

The leaves are placed alternately on the twigs, and position themselves to catch as much of the light as possible (17b and c). This means that in summer there is little light and little undergrowth in a beech wood, though bulbs can grow in the spring.

Beeches flower in May. The buds are surrounded by brown scales, which fall to the ground.

The male catkin (17b) hangs from a long stalk; the female is erect on a short stalk. A little cap encloses the two flowers, and it later bursts open into four flaps (17c). The two nuts fall out and are dispersed.

Beech wood is white and easy to split; healthy beech wood does not have a black heart. Because it is fairly hard, it is used for parquet floors and for furniture. It also makes good firewood.

17a

17d

17b

17e

17c

18. Pedunculate oak *Quercus robur*

There are oaks in Europe more than 1800 years old! Most full grown oaks reach a height of 30 m, but there is one in Scotland 39 m high.

Unlike the beech, the crown of the oak lets much light through, and mosses, herbs and shrubs grow in oak forests. The leaves (18c) appear in May, at the same time as the flowers. The male flowers are in long catkins (18b) and the few female flowers are erect on long stalks. The fruits are nuts or acorns, enclosed by a little cup at the base (18d).

The wood is very useful. It is used for boats, beams and rafters in buildings, barrels, and for furniture.

19. Sessile oak *Quercus petraea*

The pedunculate oak sheds its leaves before winter, but the sessile oak keeps its shrivelled leaves right through the winter. The leaves are a different shape from those of the pedunculate oak and have a longer stalk.

18d

18c

18b

19

18a

18e

20. Red oak *Quercus borealis*

This has been introduced from North America. It grows to a height of about 25 m. The bark is much less grooved than that of other oaks (20b). The leaves are large, and the upper side is dull green (20c); in winter they turn a beautiful red colour, especially on the young plants.

Flowering is in May. The acorn is slightly larger than in other oaks and needs two years to develop (20e). The acorn cup is smaller in size, and shallow. Although the wood is used for furniture, it is less valuable than wood from the pedunculate and sessile oaks.

20c

20e

20d

20b

20a

21. Elms

There are three main varieties of elm, and many cross-strains between them: the wych elm, *Ulmus glabra,* (A), the fluttering elm, *Ulmus laevis,* (B) and the smooth elm, *Ulmus carpinifolia,* (C). Elms are big trees with a rough scaly bark and a dense green crown.

The leaves of the wych elm are as rough as glasspaper (21 Aa). Flowering is in April, before the leaves appear. The flowers of the fluttering elm have longer stalks than those of other kinds (21Bb and 21Ab). Both stamens and pistils appear in one flower. Tiny unripe fruits can be seen long before the leaves appear, but they do not ripen until June. Each is surrounded by a wing, and is dispersed by the wind.

The wych elm is the commonest elm in Scotland, northern England and Wales; the smooth elm is commonest in the English lowlands.

21Bb

21Ab

21Ac

21Aa

B

C

23a

22b

23b

22. Hawthorn

Two kinds of hawthorn are found in Britain, the common variety, *Crataegus monogyna,* and the 'midland' variety, *Crataegus oxyacanthoides.* The common hawthorn can be either a tree or a bush. As a tree it can reach 7 m high, and it is often planted along streets.

Flowering is in May (22a) and the fruits look rather like rosehips. They are often eaten by birds, which spread the seeds with their droppings.

Other names for the hawthorn are 'may' and 'quickthorn'.

23. Rowan   *Sorbus acuparia*

The many kinds of rowan are all thornless bushes, up to 9 m high. They are sometimes called 'mountain ash' but they are not ashes. The leaves appear towards the end of April; in autumn they turn to beautiful yellow and red colours.

Flowering is in May (23b). The orange-red fruits are already ripe in August (23b), and are amongst the first fruits of autumn. The berries are eaten and the seeds are dispersed by birds.

22a

24. Medlar *Mespilus germanica*

The medlar was brought to Britain as an ornamental garden shrub, and grows up to 12 m high, but now it grows wild in south and west England.

It has many long slender branches with oval leaves, which are reddish brown when young. Flowering takes place in May. The fruits are round, red at first, and later dark purple (24b). The calyx remains on the top.

25. Bird cherry *Prunus padus*

The common bird cherry is a tree which can reach a height of 15 m. The flowers grow in long hanging clusters, and have a strong scent which attracts bees and flies (25a). The fruits are like small cherries. The fruit finally turns bluish black (25b). Birds are fond of it, but to humans it tastes sour.

The wood is fairly tough, and is used for wood carving, and for tubs and barrels.

25a

25b

24a

24b

26. Holly *Ilex aquifolium*

Holly is an evergreen, which can grow into a tree or bush 10 m high.

The leaves are hard and leathery, the upper surface dark green and the lower surface light green. The leaves on the lower branches have strong prickles (26b) but on older trees the leaves high up have no prickles (26c). Flowering is in May, but the flowers are hard to see. The fruits become bright red, and stay on the branches until the next spring (26d). Birds are very fond of the berries. We use holly as a Christmas decoration.

27. Alder buckthorn *Frangula alnus*

Several stems of this plant come out of the ground at the same place, so it is a bush, not a tree. It is hardly ever higher than 4 m (27a).

Flowering starts in June, but lasts through the summer. The flowers are greenish white (27c) and produce nectar all the time. The fruits are at first green, later red, and finally black (27d). They are eaten and spread by birds. Alder buckthorn grows in poor soil and is found as undergrowth in woodland. In the past, it was used for making charcoal.

28. Acacia *Robinia pseudoacacia*

This tree can be recognised from a distance by its dome-shaped crown (28a). The branches have thorns.

The leaves appear late—often not until June. The leaves are compound (28b), with a light green upper surface and a blue-green under-surface. The hanging flower clusters are about 10 cm long (28c); the flowers have a sweet smell, and contain much nectar. The fruits are short pods which become brown as they ripen, and stay on the tree until late into the winter (28d).

The trunk can be recognised by the deeply furrowed bark, which

forms a mesh-shaped pattern (28e). The wood is strong and long-lasting, and makes excellent beams and poles. The tree is sometimes planted in parks because of its attractive shape and the shade it gives.

28c

28a

28b

28d

28e

29. Sycamore *Acer pseudoplatanus*

Sycamores can be recognised by their leaves (29c) and their fruit (29f). They grow to a height of about 16 m. They have greyish-brown branches, with buds about 1 cm long which contain milky juice. The bark of older trees flakes off in irregular pieces (29b). The lower leaves form a 'leaf-mosaic' (29d) to catch as much light as possible.

Flowering is in May (29e). The fruits (29f), when ripe, split in two and spin to the ground.

The wood is hard and has a silky sheen. It is used for furniture, parquet floors, carving, and for making recorders and violins.

29b

29d

29e

29c

29f

29g

30. Horse chestnut *Aesculus hippocastanum*

The horse chestnut is not related to the sweet chestnut. It is a large tree, reaching 20 m in height, with an arched crown and drooping twigs (30a). On the twigs scars of fallen leaves can be seen, as well as the sticky plump buds (30b). The leaves unfold at the beginning of May, and at first they are hairy. Flowering also is in May, and the tree is full of 'candles' (30e and 30d). Not all the seeds in the big, three-celled fruits develop properly. The fruit-wall is covered with prickles; when it falls from the tree it splits and releases the chestnut brown seeds ('conkers'). They have a grey mark in the middle, where they were attached to the inside of the fruit (30f), and this is called the 'navel'.

The wood is not valuable, but the tree has been planted along many roads and in parks because it is so attractive. The tree casts a lot of shade, and is not suitable for small gardens.

31. Common lime *Tilia vulgaris*

In winter a lime can easily be recognised by its shape (31a). In summer the leaves are very dense, so it is a good tree for shade. It can reach a height of 30 m or more. Flowering is in May, (31c) and the flowers attract insects, especially bees.

The wood is good for carving, for drawing boards, bread-boards, etc, and it is also the best wood for artists' charcoal.

There are small-leaved and large-leaved varieties, but the common lime is a cross between the two. It is sometimes planted along roadsides.

32b

32d

32e

32. Ash *Fraxinus excelsior*

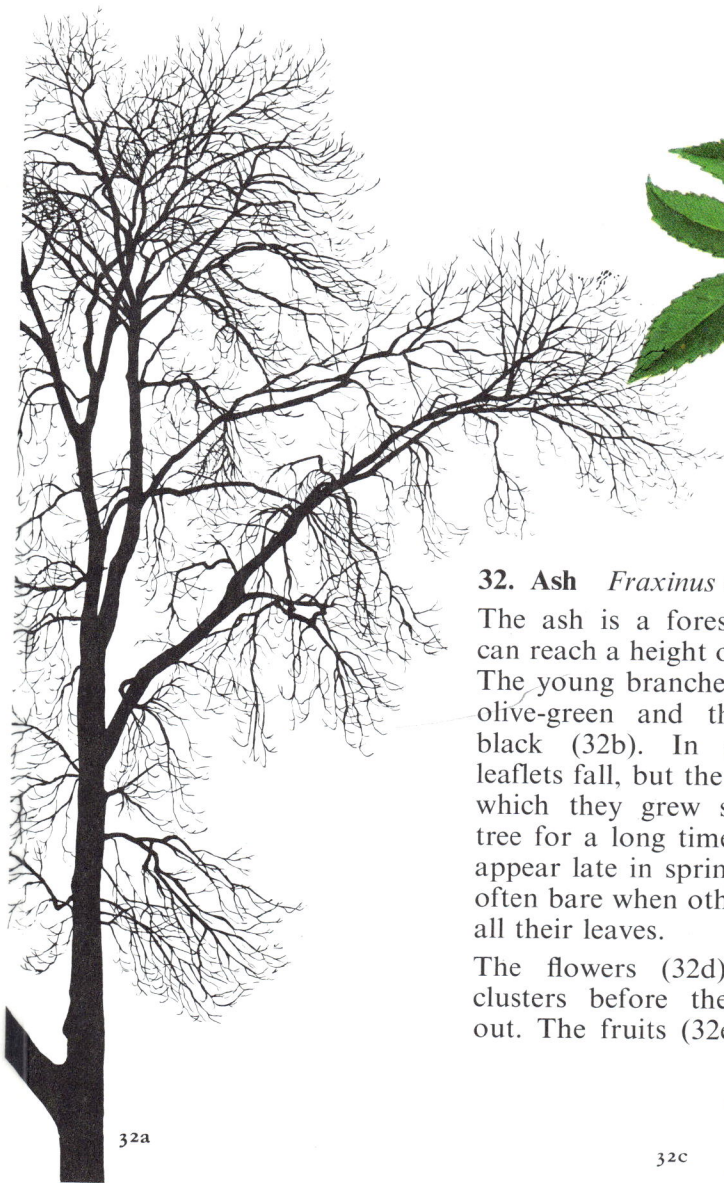

32a

The ash is a forest tree which can reach a height of 40 m (32a). The young branches are grey or olive-green and the buds are black (32b). In autumn the leaflets fall, but the leaf stalk on which they grew stays on the tree for a long time. The leaves appear late in spring—ashes are often bare when other trees have all their leaves.

The flowers (32d) appear in clusters before the leaves are out. The fruits (32e) each have a wing, so that they can be blown away by the wind.

The ash needs good soil, and does best near water. Foresters prefer the male tree, which produces more wood. The wood is easy to work and is springy, so it is suitable for handles, shafts, ladders, gymnastic apparatus, etc.

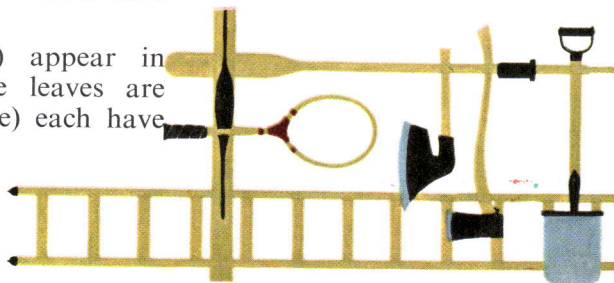

32c

33. Common elder and red-berried elder *Sambucus nigra and Sambucus racemosa*

Common elder can grow to a height of 6 m as a bush, and is sometimes almost a tree. The twigs are not woody, and contain white pith (33a). The older branches contain more wood (33b) and in the end turn brown.

The leaves (33c) unfold early. Flowering is most striking. (33d) shows the flowers of the red-berried elder; the common elder flower cluster is more out-spread. Elder berries are at first green, then red, and finally black. The fruits of the red-berried elder remain red and grow in denser clusters. Birds are very fond of them.

Elder berries are sometimes used for making wine or jam, but the fresh green parts of the elder are poisonous.

34. Guelder rose *Viburnum opulus*

This shrub can reach a height of 3 m, and is often planted in gardens and parks. The outer flowers cannot produce fruit, though they are large and attract insects. The inner flowers are smaller but they produce the red fruits. All parts of the plant are poisonous to man.

Wood

Uses of wood

Firewood

Very little wood is now used as firewood. First coal, then later oil, gas and electricity, have taken the place of wood as a fuel.

The result is that wood-gathering, which was once a common activity, is no longer worth while. Chopping, sawing and piling up wood takes time, so now there is often a good deal of pruned and lopped wood lying around in woodland. People are now trying to think of new uses for this wood, which is at present going to waste.

Thinnings

Wood obtained by thinning and pruning is still used by market-gardeners and farmers for light fencing, beanstalks, etc, but even this is beginning to take more time to gather than it is worth.

Timber

Heavier wood of good quality is used for sawing into planks, poles, beams, etc.

Wood for industry

Much wood comes into a category between timber and thinnings, and this can be used for all sorts of things. The best quality woods are used for making plywood, and laminated wood for furniture. Shavings and chips are made into chipboard and hardboard. These are useful because they do not shrink.

Wood pulp is boiled with chemicals, and is separated into lignin and cellulose. These are used to make paper, plastics, rayon and explosives.

Stacks of wood for industrial use

Annual rings

When a tree trunk is cut across, we can see rings in the wood, in smaller and smaller circles as they get nearer to the middle. Each year that the tree grows, it adds one light band and one dark band to its girth. The light band is wood grown in the early spring, and the dark band is wood grown in the summer. One light band and one dark band together make an annual ring. After September the tree scarcely grows until the next spring.

If we count the dark bands from the centre to the outside, we can tell the age of the tree. We can also see, from the thickness of the ring for a particular year, how well the tree grew in that year. This in turn tells us what the weather was like. Because trees can live sometimes for over a century, we can study the weather conditions over a long period of time.

Patterns in sawn wood

When the trunk is cut across, we can also see fine lines running from the centre out towards the bark. These are called *medullary rays*. These are transport channels, which carry food and water in a radial (sideways) direction, for example from the centre outwards. When a trunk is stripped bare of bark, we can see them 'end-on' as oval marks.

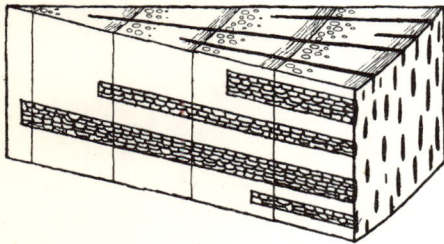

Medullary rays

If the trunk has been sawn lengthwise into planks, then a plank which comes from near the centre of the cylinder will show both the lengthwise stripes of the growth rings and the crosswise stripes of medullary rays. All other planks show grain. Grain marks are more or less parallel if the trunk was exactly straight, but more often the grain is curved. Between the grain lines we can sometimes see the marks where the medullary rays were sawn through.

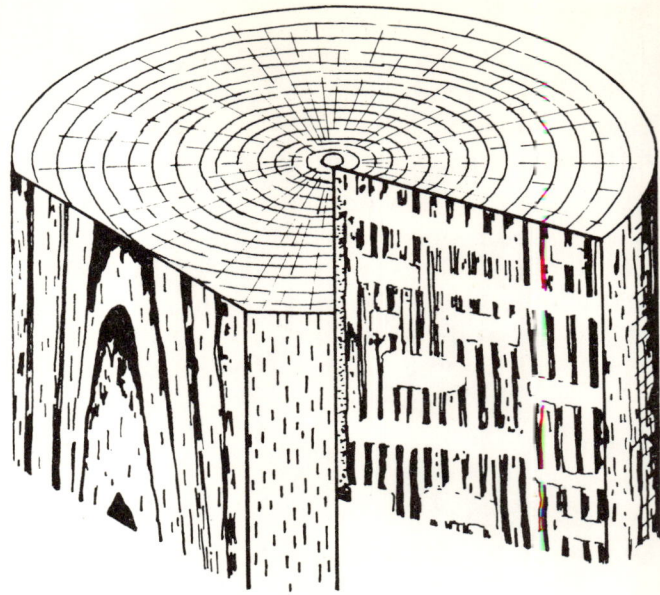

Patterns in wood

Structure of trunks and branches

A trunk is a woody stem, and a branch is a woody side stalk. They become woody over the years. The stem of a seedling is sappy, not hard. Herbaceous plants never become woody, but trees and shrubs do. Trees and bushes reach much greater heights than herbaceous plants, so they need firmness in their stems and branches.

A cross section of a trunk or branch shows a variety of tissues. From the outside to the centre, these are:

a *the bark*, which dies off on the outside; it is water repellent;

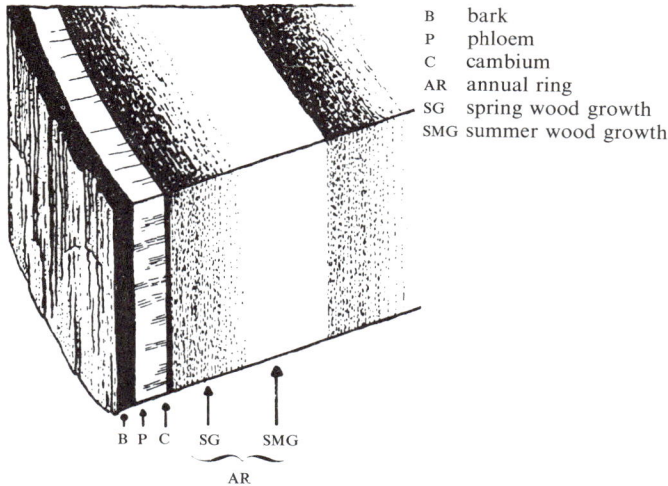

B	bark
P	phloem
C	cambium
AR	annual ring
SG	spring wood growth
SMG	summer wood growth

A section through a trunk

b the bast or phloem: transport of foodstuffs takes place here;
c the cambium: this is the growth layer, and the cells here divide and multiply;
d wood with dying and dead cells: upward transport of water, which carries mineral salts, take place here;
e the pith at the centre of the trunk or branch, often so squashed as to be invisible.

How trees and shrubs feed

Below you can see a simplified diagram of how a tree functions. Using the sun's energy, the green leaves take in carbon dioxide from the air. At the same time there is movement of liquids in two directions, mainly water and mineral salts up through the wood to the leaves, and water with dissolved sugars downwards towards the roots. There is also a radial movement of liquids along the medullary rays.

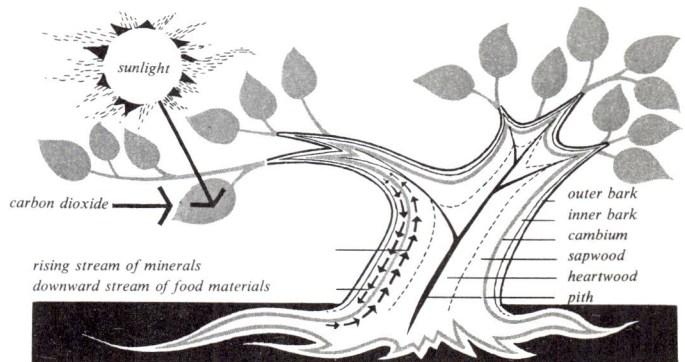

How a tree functions

Ways of using wood

A CONIFERS

B DECIDUOUS TREES

wood for industry   timber   round blocks   quarter blocks   timber   firewood

paper
cardboard
matches
veneer
hardboard
softboard
rayon
lacquer
glue
turpentine
resin
tar
vanilla
acetic acids
acetates
paint brushes
alcohol
lamp-black
charcoal
pencils
perfumes
nail varnish

Man and forest

Treeless regions

The polar regions and the tops of mountains are treeless because they are too cold for trees to grow. In Britain few trees grow above 600 m. The deserts are bare because of lack of water, and some coastal or mountainous areas are too exposed to winds.

Disturbance by man

Unfortunately man has often caused the destruction of forests. The prairies of North America were once covered with forest, but too much felling and burning has destroyed them. Sometimes the climate has changed as a result. Iceland is a typical example; its huge forests were felled by earlier inhabitants and no new trees were planted. Now the land is treeless, storms can blow freely across it and the soil is less fertile, because the topsoil has been blown or washed away.

Disturbance by animals

In other places animals have caused deforestation. In Ireland sheep have done immeasurable damage, and the island of St Helena has been eaten completely bare by the descendants of a few imported goats.

Primeval forest

In prehistoric times Britain was a well-wooded country. In southern England the main forest tree was the pedunculate oak, but in the higher lands of the north and west, in Wales and in the Scottish Highlands the sessile oak was more common. Over much of the Highlands the main tree was the Scots pine.

Cultivated forests

Very little of the primeval forest has survived; it was cleared by the early British farmers and later by the Saxons, and in Scotland by the Norse settlers. Some forests were preserved in both kingdoms for royal hunting (the New Forest, Sherwood, Epping) and even re-planted, but most royal lands were gradually sold to great landowners, who cut down the timber.

In England some of the landowners planted new trees, often in coppices and along hedgerows rather than in woods or forests. New trees were introduced—hornbeam, sweet chestnut, sycamore, larch, spruce and other new conifers.

The Forestry Commission

We import 90% of the wood we use in Britain and we have less forest land than almost any other European country. During the 1914–18 and 1939–45 wars, when it was hard to import timber, much of our woodland had to be cut down, and in 1919 the Government set up the Forestry Commission to improve the situation. The commission buys about 22 000 hectares (55 000 acres) of land each year for new planting (afforestation). Vast areas of land in the Scottish Highlands, in northern England and Wales, which have been nearly useless for many years, are now planted with young forests—and in fifty years we shall reap the full benefits.

Pruning young conifers

These new forests also help by providing work near their homes for men who would otherwise have had to move into towns to look for work. Paper and pulp mills have been built, which also provide jobs.

The Forestry Commission also tries to help us use and appreciate our forests for recreation.

What the foresters do

The Forestry Commission buys land which has been used for rough grazing. The foresters use tractors to plough and drain the land and then plant the small trees, usually about 1·5 m apart.

A great deal of thought is given to choosing the best kind of tree. Rainfall, temperature, exposure to wind, soil, all affect the decision. Most of the trees planted now are conifers, because they grow faster and are more economical than other trees.

In a day, one man can plant about 1000 small trees, which have been grown in a nursery until they are 15 to 20 cm high. A fence is needed around the plantation to keep out animals, especially rabbits and deer, but cows and sheep can also destroy the young trees.

Very little weeding is necessary for the first two years, but the trees have to be carefully protected from damage by insects and fungi. The greatest danger is the fire risk, and stacks of brooms are left at the side of forest tracks for beating out fires. Lorries with special water tanks are ready at all times, and in places there are fire-watch towers to spot the first sign of smoke.

The trees need some pruning after about six years, and after twenty years the wood is 'thinned'. The poorer trees are cut down to give the better trees more chance to grow, and the felled trees are sold, mostly for pulp. It takes fifty years before even a fast-growing tree is usable as timber and eighty to a hundred years before it will make good timber.

Visiting forests

The Forestry Commission has created seven Forest Parks in areas of magnificent scenery —Argyll, Glen Trool, Glen More, the Queen Elizabeth Forest Park in the Trossachs, the Forest of Dean, Snowdonia and the Border Forest Park. These have camping sites, footpaths and guidebooks, and are worth visiting if you can reach them.

But over sixty other forests now have 'forest trails' for walkers who want to study wild-life and trees, and there are a number of nature reserves in forests where animals can be seen in their natural surroundings.

The Forestry Commission is very helpful in supplying information, if you tell them exactly what you want to know about.

Because of the fire-risk, it is by far the best to leave matches and cigarette lighters at home when you are going to a forest. *Never* light camp fires.

Schools and forests

Some schools have adopted their own plot of forest, and grown trees on it. Any school near one of the Commission's forests can apply for a small plot, and work it themselves. The local forester's advice has to be followed, and it does mean a lot of hard work!

The Commission is also prepared to give young trees to schools for planting in the school grounds or playing fields, so even if you do not live in the country you may be able to grow your own tree.

Before land can be planted with trees, it has to be drained

Tree flowers

Trees such as the hawthorn and horse chestnut have very large and conspicuous flowers, but others have very tiny ones. These flowers may be found in cones or catkins and can often be seen before the leaves appear.

Most herbaceous plants have male parts (stamens) and female parts (pistils) in the same flower, but in many trees they are in separate cones, e.g. pine (1) and larch (3), or in separate flowers, e.g. elm (21) and beech (17), or even on separate trees, e.g. holly (26) and willow (10). These flowers are so small that few people notice them and very few of them have any petals. The male flowers often consist only of a scale leaf with a few stamens which produce the pollen. The female flower may be just a single pistil.

Before any seeds can be formed, the pollen grains must reach the pistil and they may be carried there by wind or insects. The pollen then fertilises the ovules in the part of the pistil called the ovary and the seeds are formed. The rest of the ovary usually forms part of the fruit.

When ripe, the fruits are dispersed by wind or animals and some of the seeds inside them grow into new plants and eventually into trees.

The catkins and female flowers of a walnut, Juglans regia

Common terms

LEAF-SHAPES

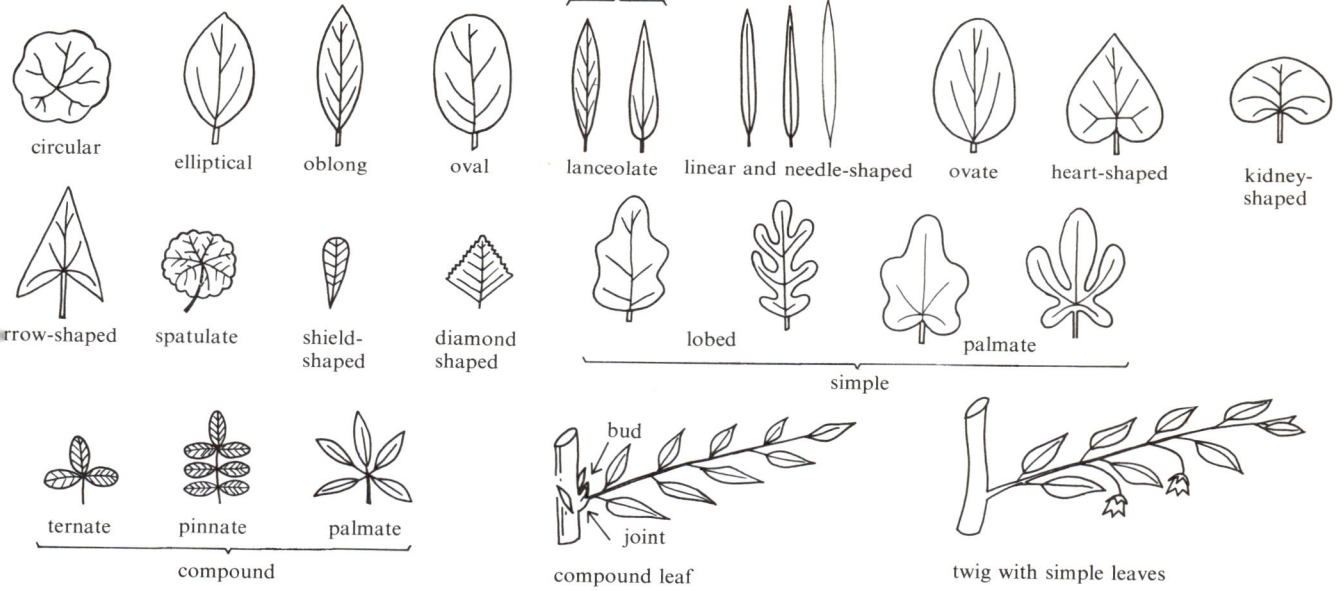

circular   elliptical   oblong   oval   lanceolate   linear and needle-shaped   ovate   heart-shaped   kidney-shaped

arrow-shaped   spatulate   shield-shaped   diamond shaped   lobed   palmate

simple

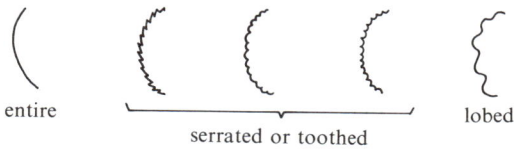

ternate   pinnate   palmate

compound

bud

joint

compound leaf

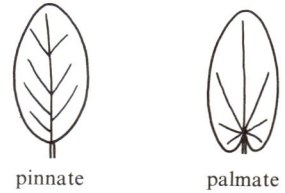

twig with simple leaves

LEAF MARGINS

entire   serrated or toothed   lobed

LEAF VEINS

pinnate   palmate

LEAF ARRANGEMENTS

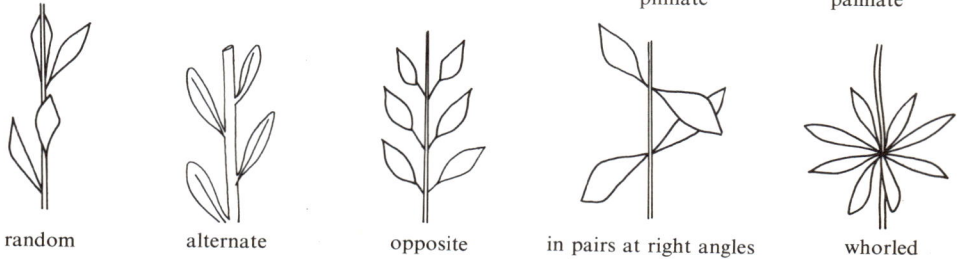

random   alternate   opposite   in pairs at right angles   whorled

Other books about trees

Wayside and woodland trees, HL Edlin
   (Warne)
Your book of trees, M Hadfield (Faber)
Everyman's wild flowers and trees,
   M Hadfield (Dent)
Pocket guide to trees in Britain,
   AW Holbrook (Country life)
British trees and shrubs, RD Meikle
   (Eyre & Spottiswoode)
Trees and bushes in wood and hedgerow,
   H Vedel and J Lange (Methuen)
Observer's book of trees, WJ Stokoe,
   (Warne)
Identification of trees and shrubs, FK Makins
   (Dent)

The Forestry Commission publishes a number
of books and leaflets. A full list of their
publications can be obtained free from: The
Forestry Commission, 25 Savile Row,
London W1X 2AY, or: The Forestry
Commission, 25 Drumsheugh Gardens,
Edinburgh 3.

Index

Index of Latin names

21117576U

75